To You Wherever You Are

An Unlikely Courier Delivers God's Message of Hope

WRITTEN BY

SUE CONOVER

A Sue Conover Book published by Conover Publishing

P.O. Box 359
Aurora Ohio, 44202

Printed in the United States of America 24 23 22 2120 19 18 17 16
1 2 3 4 5 6

ISBN-13 (Printed Version): 978-0-9980330-2-0
Ebook: 978-0-9980330-5-1

Illustrations created by Sue Conover and Pam Moore
Editing by Jana L. Good of Good Life Coaching, LLC.
Cover and Interior Design by Jesus Cordero of Anointing Productions

Table Of Content

Introduction

This is a true story that may seem stranger than fiction. That's what happens when God is in charge of the events. You will learn that no matter what you are going through in your life right now, God has not left you to fight your battles alone. God's plan is to show you His unfailing love for you and His mighty power to deliver and save today, just the same as He did in the Bible. He uses this story to illustrate this truth.

Cruelty and violence are all around us. Our real enemy is unrelenting, and we have all been touched by the violence he inspires to one degree or another. Many of us have personally experienced violence in our lives or know someone who has been touched by it.

Violence and abuse are realities of our world today. Much of the time it is unexplainable and unjust, and it always leaves people wounded and broken, feeling hopeless and ashamed and powerless to overcome.

God wants to show you that your simple prayer can unleash all the heavenly power needed to crush your enemies and deliver you. He wants to show you a way when it seems there is none, and He desires to move on your behalf in the most unexpected and miraculous ways.

1

A Heart Cry

This story began on Tuesday morning, May 12, 2016, in Aurora, Ohio. The day started like many others, with a prayer: "God, do You know where I am? Do You see me?" My life seemed such a sharp contrast to that warm, sunny spring day. The Lord had moved me to this new location, a little apartment with a small pond nearby. A new chapter in my life was unfolding with a journey into uncharted waters. I was seeking His comfort and the reassurance that He was indeed still right by my side.

Little did I know that God was getting ready to answer my prayer that morning through a little mallard duck. This is her story.

But ask the animals, and they will teach you, or the birds in the sky, and they will tell you; . . . Which of all these does not know that the hand of the LORD has done this? (Job 12:7-9, NIV)

There is a small, peaceful pond near where I live. It is surrounded by green grass and woods with tall, sturdy trees. I can see it from my dining room window. There are mallard ducks that call this place home. The female ducks come every spring and make nests in the nearby woods and sit on their eggs for about 28 days until the ducklings hatch. The location of the nest is very important, because the babies are vulnerable to many predators, such as raccoons and owls and hawks and even neighborhood cats. That May morning, a little mallard duck and ten of her newly hatched ducklings arrived at the pond; this was the first time I had seen them. I named her Ava, the Latin word for duck. Under Ava's watchful eyes, the sweet ducklings swam and explored their new world. Each night Ava would take her babies back to the nest in the woods.

On Thursday morning, Ava came to the pond with four ducklings. By Saturday, there were only three left. Seven of the ducklings had fallen prey during the night to one of their many predators.

Created by God, they were given life and turned over to Ava to care for, teach, and watch over. Each duck, like each of us, is given an exact number of days, as God determines the time they will spend here on Earth. It made me sad to see that the ducklings didn't survive, but I must put my trust in the Lord, that He has all the answers to life's hard questions. He planned for all of them to be a part of this story, a story that would be read and would minister to many people. He knows the why for seven of them, why their part in the story only lasted for so few days. I know that everything God creates has eternal value and purpose and cannot be measured in the number of days given.

Creation and God's creatures are so raw and wild. They can seem harsh and cruel but they all glorify their Creator with simple trust during the days He gives them. These creatures depend on His loving care without questioning, unlike us humans.

On Sunday, a pack of rogue mallard ducks showed up. There were five of them and they started ganging up on Ava. They held her down with their beaks, holding onto her wings and pinning her down by her neck and attacking her. I tried to chase them away and threw small stones near them to startle them. I spent the next three days patrolling the pond, day and evening, chasing the five ducks away. The fourth day, Ava left in the afternoon before they came and hid herself and her ducklings in her nest in the woods. She was learning to take steps to protect herself and her ducklings.

I called the Animal Protective League and County Metro Parks Services, asking about relocating this little family before Ava was injured or killed, but they told me that they were unable to help her. They informed me that this happens sometimes, that a group of rogue ducks will attack in a pack. Ava would not fly away to protect herself and escape the abuse because she wouldn't leave her precious ducklings. In this I was witnessing the evil effects of sin reaching into all of creation. There are bullies and evil attacks even among animals.

The next day, a second female mallard duck showed up at the pond with twelve ducklings. She was vulnerable and fell victim to the same attacks by this pack of rogue ducks. When they went after her, however, she quickly took flight to escape, leaving her ducklings, but she returned to them a few minutes later. All the while, Ava watched.

The next time the pack tried to attack Ava, she also took flight and escaped.

She was shown a way of escape and had new victories over her attackers. She had been equipped with wings right there on her back the whole time, but she feared for her babies' safety while she was gone. The answer had been there all the time; she just needed to believe and let go of her fears. She grew in experience and knowledge and was quickly learning to deal with the giants in her life. She must have moved her nest in the woods to a safer place because the three ducklings remained alive and grew stronger each new day.

God promises us, "Do not fear, for I am with you: do not be dismayed, for I am your God. I will strengthen you and help you" (Isaiah 41:10, NIV).

God used me to help this duck and her ducklings for a little while, as she learned to navigate this new experience and terrible situation. For the next week, the five ducks would arrive, and Ava would fly away, and they would fly after her. Her ducklings would huddle together and wait for her to return. This went on morning, afternoon, and evening if she was at the pond. I was getting weary and discouraged trying to be vigilant in chasing these ducks away from Ava. The other more experienced female duck with the twelve ducklings came to the pond some days, but she spent most days hiding out in the woods with her babies to avoid these rogue ducks.

> He will deliver the needy who cry out,
> the afflicted who have no one to help.
> (Psalm 72:12, NIV)

I have learned over time that my part in trial is to hold on to my faith, believe that God is with me and will rescue me, and put my hope in Him when everything looks hopeless.

The next night I prayed and asked God to help this little duck somehow. "Send an angel, if You would, unless they only come to help people." I told God, "You said in Your Word that Your eyes are on the sparrow."

2

God's Amazing Rescue

had observed over the past few days a single black raven hanging around the pond. I wondered where he had come from and why he too was alone. Ravens always travel in groups. Then I worried that he had noticed Ava leaving her babies all the time and flying away. Maybe he was waiting for an opportunity to snatch one of the babies, as these birds are carnivorous. This black raven had witnessed the frequent attacks on Ava and me chasing the five ducks away.

The following morning, I heard the ducks and went out to chase them away as usual. I gathered some stones from the edge of the water and headed to the far end of the pond. The five ducks had Ava pinned down on the bank with several holding down her wings with their beaks and one pinning her by the neck. As I approached, something happened that I struggled to believe, even though I was witnessing it with my own eyes.

The black raven swooped down from the sky and landed right on the back of the leader of the rogue ducks. This big raven started to viciously peck at the duck until it let go of Ava and she was able to fly away. And it didn't end there. The five ducks flew after Ava, but the black raven flew after them. I stood and watched as it attacked the rogue ducks in the sky as they flew. Ava landed back on the bank where her ducklings were waiting, the five other ducks right behind her.

With the raven beside her, she suddenly had the confidence to face her attackers. The big raven puffed up his chest and opened his wings. They both started fighting and pecking at her attackers, face to face. The raven was in full combat mode, pecking, lunging, and pushing his full weight into the rogue ducks with great force. His attack was relentless, and his razor-sharp beak caused puncture wounds that I could see on the chest of one of the attackers. Ava was right beside the raven, puffing out her chest and fighting with all her might. This went on for several minutes as I watched in disbelief. The fighting finally ended with the five ducks giving up and flying away. The raven stayed close by the little duck family for the rest of that day.

I was having a hard enough time processing these events that evening, and then I suddenly remembered what I had talked to the Lord about the night before. I had asked Him, "Could You dispatch an angel to defend a duck, or are angels only sent to help humans?" His answer was in living color before my very eyes in this supernatural rescue. It made me think about a story in the Bible of a raven that was dispatched to help a prophet named Elijah.

Then the word of the LORD came to Elijah: "Leave here, turn eastward and hide in the Kerith Ravine, east of the Jordan. You will drink from the brook, and I have directed the ravens to supply you with food there." So, he did what the LORD had told him. He went to the Kerith Ravine, east of the Jordan, and stayed there. The ravens brought him bread and meat in the morning and bread and meat in the evening, and he drank from the brook. (1 Kings 17:2-6, NIV)

All events on Earth are under God's control and He even uses animals to function as divine agents and help fulfill His missions. Ravens would not naturally feed humans, but they fed Elijah at God's command. My simple heartfelt prayer to God was heard and answered—and in no ordinary way! He answered in such an amazing way that only He could receive the glory for it.

Literally overnight, the whole picture changed. Ava showed up at the pond with her three ducklings, as did the five rogue ducks. However, now the five ducks were intimidated by *her*. When one of the rogue ducks came near her, she would charge at it, causing it to flee in fear. Even stranger, if several members of the pack swam together toward Ava, she would charge at them to attack them but they would turn on one another, fighting each other in confusion.

Now, these rogue ducks were very fearful and unsure of themselves and their unity seemed to be broken. Ava, however, had become fearless! She would go after all five ducks at the same time and wouldn't back down until they had fled. She had learned to overcome her enemies, have confidence in herself, and believe in herself.

This is the goal for all of us. God doesn't want us to stay victims. He loves us too much to just fix everything for us, leaving us immature and constantly under attack. He wants to teach us to have victory over our enemies and become strong and brave warriors. God is so proud of this little duck! She had learned in two weeks to be victorious and rule over her enemies.

Ava stayed at the pond all summer and into the fall season. Her ducklings grew up and I had the joy of watching them learn to fly. It was amazing to watch as the ducklings spent weeks flapping and lifting their bodies off the ground until their wings were finally strong enough to lift them off the ground to fly away. They did pretty well right away with the takeoff. However, the real challenge was the landing. It took months for these ducks to successfully land on the ground or in the pond. I watched as they landed on their face or chest and tumbled and rolled down the hill toward the water, coming down too soon. There were other times when they landed in the water but went headfirst underwater because they came down too sharply. I never realized that ducks had to struggle so hard to master the art of flying. Once again, I was learning something from these wonderful creatures. We all start out weak and inexperienced in the skills we will need to survive and thrive. All of life is about learning and growing.

The pond had become a peaceful place and other mallard ducks came to enjoy it and spend the warm summer days swimming and playing and resting along its quiet shores.

As I struggle with my own giants coming against me, I see how God worked to help this little duck get through a boot-camp experience in life as a young adult and new mom. He didn't just step in and fix it, but like a good father trains a grown child, He was there with her, showing and giving her tools to succeed in life. He taught her to step into this new role and grow in maturity and strength. There was always a limit to what her attackers could do, how far they could go. Through this trial and difficult learning experience, she came out a real warrior.

I could identify with this little duck so much. I too was going through a severe trial and overwhelming experience that I thought

I was totally inexperienced and ill equipped to handle. I was under extreme attack emotionally and spiritually. I was praying hard, but I was struggling to trust God and hold on to my faith.

Throughout my childhood journey, there was an unwelcomed and uninvited travel companion: abuse. The enemy's plan was to steal, kill and destroy me. He wanted to inflict as many wounds in my soul and spirit as he could, to kill my dreams and destroy and stamp out all hope for my future.

As I entered my adult years and I married and had children, I thought that finally I had escaped my childhood companion: abuse.

I soon discovered that this unwelcome companion of my childhood had followed me, and the enemy's plan was still the same: to steal, kill and destroy me. I struggled for many years with questions about why the Lord allows so much suffering.

In the trials and struggles that I experienced in life, I prayed and thought that God should step in and change my circumstances and defeat all my enemies for me right away! Over time He showed me that His plan was not to take me out of the trials but to take me through them. As with Ava, He loved me too much to fix everything and leave me weak and immature. The Lord has brought me such a long way, and I am learning to have real victory in the midst of very difficult circumstances, just like Ava.

This little drama that was taking place outside my window was God showing me His amazing care and provision for Ava, just a little mallard duck. In this world, we will have trials and tribulation. God has promised to rescue us from every evil attack and bring us safely into His heavenly kingdom. When we go through deep water, He will be with us. We will not drown. And when we walk through the fire, we won't be destroyed. He is in the process of maturing and growing our faith. God didn't promise to prevent all evil attacks, nor did He promise that we would never get our feet wet or experience the deep flood waters of trial and suffering. He did promise to be with us in the midst of the storms, rescue us out of them, and carry us to safety.

He will take pity on the weak and the needy and save the needy from death. He will rescue them from oppression and violence. (Psalm 72:13-14, NIV)

Many times, I have prayed, "God, don't let me have to go through the flood and flames." When they come, I have gotten mad at God and said to Him, "You didn't keep Your promises to me." But He never promised to prevent trials from coming. God is faithful, and He promised to be with me in trouble, to rescue me, and to bring me through to safety.

WHY?

WHY?

WHY?

WHY?

WHY?

There is a bigger story in the heavenly places and bigger battles to be waged in the spirit realm. The stories in the Bible are both about real events on Earth and about the battles that are fought in the heavens against God's spiritual enemies. The stakes are much higher, and we fight against principalities and powers of darkness, against Satan's armies. We learn through our trials here on Earth how to fight the bigger battles through prayer and intercession, and by using our spiritual armor and weapons—mighty through God!—to pull down strongholds and demons. God is teaching us to be warriors to defeat our enemies.

Jesus defeated Satan at the cross, but Satan continues to fight his eviction from territory he has comfortably occupied in our lives for so long. The devil wants to prevent us from learning who we are and from taking the power and authority God has given us—all power and authority over the devil, in the name of Jesus. The devil wants to keep us in captivity and bondage through his lies and intimidation, but Jesus said, "You will know the truth, and the truth will set you free" (John 8:32, NIV).

3

The Truth

The truth that the Lord wants you to know and come to believe is that He loves you! The good news is that Jesus came to seek and save the lost, to heal the brokenhearted, to proclaim freedom for the captives and release for the prisoners who have been held in darkness by the devil. He wants you to experience His presence and power and to walk in His love, while ruling and reigning victoriously over your enemy.

If we endure, we will also reign with him. (2 Timothy 2:12, NIV)

This story unfolded for this little duck so that I could watch and be encouraged and, in turn, encourage you. God knows each of us intimately and longs to speak to you and tell you stories about who He really is and how much He loves you. I urge you to let Him come into the tender places in your heart and tell you a story; let Him reveal Himself to you and work the impossible beyond what you could believe or imagine.

What little pond do you find yourself in, alone and isolated and fighting for your life? Are you convinced that your story is unimportant to God and that He doesn't see you? That He would never come to where you are? I want you to remember this little duck. Perhaps you are saying that you don't know how to pray. Remember that this duck didn't speak. She didn't do anything to merit or deserve such love, care, and divine intervention from God.

God has put it on my heart to tell you this duck's story to inspire you and encourage you to look to Him so that He can show His love and faithfulness to you. God is big enough and God is strong enough to fight for you. He desires to help you.

God sent His Son to die on the cross to prove His love. He was raised to life so that He could bring hope and life to all men. God doesn't want us to live in fear, doubt, and hopelessness.

I love that God used this little duck's story to speak to us. I could write a book about all the amazing things God has done for me: dramatic rescues, supernatural deliverance, so many healing touches, and all His love, care and faithfulness to me. But God, in His wisdom, chose to use this duck's story because He knew you might have been tempted to think that there was something that I did to get God to hear and help me. Wherever you are right now, you can call upon the name of the Lord Jesus and He will hear you—and He will answer you. He loves you and knows just where you are!

About the Author

The creator of this true story is God. The message of God's stories are always about His unfailing and unconditional love and His power to deliver and save us. I believe the reason God chose me to write this story is so that you would see that it was not any creative skills or any experience that I had to offer. He wanted you to know that it came from Him. I am a retired nurse, and the only writing that I have done are nurses notes in patient charts and an occasional letter to a friend. Then, just so there would be no doubt about the author of this story, He chose someone like me, with no technical or computer skills. In fact, I don't even have a computer in my home. I have worked on this book at the Solon branch of the Cuyahoga Public Library, with the help of the patient and supportive library staff there. God took care of every detail, one step at a time. My hope is that this will inspire you to write about a story that God has put on your heart. Maybe you have been thinking that you don't have the resources or skill to write a book. I am living proof that God is able to accomplish His plan through anyone He chooses, independent of resources or skills you may or may not have. If you are thinking that you are too old to begin such a huge undertaking as writing a book, then you should know that I am 70 years old and this is my first book. God truly "is able to [carry out His purpose and] do superabundantly more than all that we dare ask or think [infinitely beyond our greatest prayers, hopes, or dreams], according to His power that is at work within us" (Ephesians 3:20, The Amplified Bible).

CPSIA information can be obtained
at www.ICGtesting.com
Printed in the USA
BVHW010441200219
540698BV00006B/27/P